THE
Archive Photographs
SERIES

BRADFORD

Tyrrell Street, near Town Hall Square, *c.* 1920. The end of Thornton Road is on the extreme left of the picture.

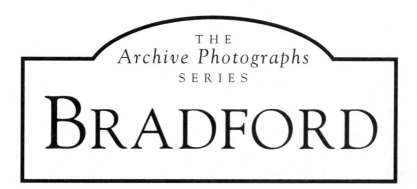

THE
Archive Photographs
SERIES

BRADFORD

Compiled by
Dr. Gary Firth

CHALFORD

First published 1995
Copyright © Dr. Gary Firth, 1995

The Chalford Publishing Company
St Mary's Mill, Chalford,
Stroud, Gloucestershire, GL6 8NX

ISBN 0 7524 0321 4

Typesetting and origination by
The Chalford Publishing Company
Printed in Great Britain by
Redwood Books, Trowbridge

In memory of David James

Contents

'Laikin Aht' in a courtyard near the bottom of Leeds Road, 1900. For many Bradford children this meant going through the ritual of some favourite game or song. Here, the oldest child excludes an unwanted boy and reminds the others of the rules. A delightful reminiscence of childhood.

Introduction

Although Bradford has a history going back well over a thousand years, the pictures in this book date from mid-Victorian times when the town was a *locus classicus* of urban-industrial growth. It had changed from a small West Yorkshire market town, which in 1801 had a population of 13,264, to the seventh largest city in Britain fifty years later, with a population of 103,778. By approving Bradford's Charter of Incorporation in April 1847, a young Queen Victoria began a momentous chapter in the history of this prosperous and rapidly-growing community.

Bradford's wealth and expansion had been achieved at some considerable social cost, however, as large numbers of people worked long hours for unremunerative pay, living in an environment that closely resembled the shanty towns of the American West. In 1844 a government official, James Smith, declared it to be 'the most filthy town I ever visited' and a year later, a young German visitor found himself in 'a dark alley of an evil-smelling town – we are in Bradford!' All those who lived and worked in the town suffered from its environmental degeneration and from the widespread pollution of its natural resources of fresh air and water.

However, in 1847 Bradford became a municipal corporation run by its own elected council and, from that time forward, the quality of urban life began to improve owing to a perfect blend of private enterprise and municipal initiative. In place of the squalor and filth of an unregulated town there arose, phoenix-like, a solid well-planned Victorian city with its architectural gems at the Wool Exchange, Kirkgate Market, St George's Hall, Court Houes, Little Germany, and that study in civic pride – the Bradford Town Hall. We must not forget, of course, the numerous mills and factories, whose industry had made all the previously mentioned buildings possible, as well as the hundreds of rows of terraced houses (some back-to-back). Bradford, by 1900, was one of the finest provincial towns of Victorian England, fiercely independent of London in its politics and with a rich cultural tradition, particularly in music and social welfare.

Contemporary with the rebuilding of the town after 1847 came the invention of the camera. Early photographs enable us to see Bradford and its townfolk as they were, at work, at play, at prayer, at school and at their daily routines in and around a town which saw the passing of royalty, two world wars, and two major depressions in the worsted industry.

It is in the nature of towns to change, and Bradford is no exception to that rule. The high watermark of growth and prosperity was reached before the end of the Great War and the popularity of the motor car after the Second World War forced upon the city fathers a massive reconstruction plan for the centre of the city (city status had been conferred in 1897). A re-vamped central area was to be surrounded by an outer ring road and an inner civic ring road.

The plan, devised by S.G. Wardley, City Engineer and Surveyor, was to give Bradford a new skyline and 'cityscape', removing many of the old landmarks featured in the photographs in this book. Wardley and his plan are not without their critics. Many in Bradford today view the city centre as a dispiriting and depressing place, where dark and occasionally dangerous subways offer uneasy sanctuary from the traffic-congested roads with their concrete flyovers and underpasses. Specialist and familiar shops (victims of runaway rents) have been forced to close and have been replaced by a never-ending tide of takeaways and cheap gift shops. Popular public houses have given way to designer bistros, and cinemas have been demolished to make way for car parks. In order to improve Bradford now it would be naïve to try to go back in time and match the splendid burst of civic pride of 150 years ago. That change was born of massive surplus wealth and a denial of poverty and hardship for those at the foot of the social ladder. Such a world has long since passed. Solutions to Bradford's urban programme will require the co-operation of collective agencies and private enterprise working alongside each other. Meanwhile, it might be instructive for those in charge of the city's future to look at the photographs in this book and see the high standards in public building and community living set by Bradford's late Victorian and Edwardian citizens and for the rest of us to recapture the atmosphere and flavour of this unique Yorkshire city in its various stages of transition.

Gary Firth
Bradford & Ilkley Community College
July, 1995

Canal Road, 1956. A view eastwards across the city towards Manningham (in the top right of the photograph).

One
Old Bradford

a Painting in the possession of
Mr. John Cunton

BRADFORD IN 1835.

Painted by Wilson

Bradford from the north west in 1835. This view across the valley is taken from a large oil painting by J. Wilson Anderson. It shows the old town situated in a natural amphitheatre of rolling hills and green pastures, its streets running between the tower of the ancient parish Church (left) and the more modern structure of Christ Church (right) at the top of Darley Street.

Kirkgate, *c.* 1800. This is taken from a series of water-colour paintings by N.S. Crichton in 1870/80. Kirkgate was one of the three ancient highways, making up the medieval settlement of Bradford and leading to the parish church. To the left of this picture can be seen the Piece Hall (1773), built for the sale of worsted pieces and spun yarn made in the local cottage industry. Adjoining the Piece Hall is the original Talbot Hotel.

Bull's Head Inn, *c.* 1790. This public house was to be found at the bottom of Westgate, where butchers publicly slaughtered beasts and sold the meat from their open stalls. In front of the inn was the bull ring, where bull baiting was a popular sport. The picture also shows Bradford's ancient pillory, where miscreants were held up to public ridicule.

Christ Church, c. 1830. As mentioned earlier, this Anglican church was located at the top of Darley Street. It had been built in 1813 on an area which was then essentially rural and on land donated by Benjamin Rawson, Lord of the Manor. Bradford's urban sprawl compelled the building's demolition in 1879. The picture shows the official Bradford Fair – an occasion for pleasure rather than commerce. Here were wild beasts, waxworks, travelling thespians, magicians, fortune tellers, quack doctors and cheapjacks – all the fun of the fair.

Paper Hall, c. 1800. This imposing yeoman's residence was built in 1643 by William Rookes of Royds Hall, Low Moor. Bradford historian John James described it as being in a 'miserable state of dilapidation and neglect' in 1841. A recent and extensive programme of rebuilding has rescued it from oblivion.

These are two of the town's ancient hostelries. The Bowling Green Hotel could be found in
Bridge Street. It had been rebuilt in 1750 and thereafter ranked as the best inn of the town,
offering unlimited accommodation for man and beast. Another eighteenth-century tavern was
the New Inn, well known for its spacious stabling and as a venue for the weekly pig market.

The Sun Hotel. This water-colour by Crichton shows the hotel at the bottom of Ivegate (right) in its heyday as a coaching inn. It was by far the most important inn of pre-industrial Bradford and was noted for its dancing assemblies and social occasions. It hosted the start of numerous commercial and industrial schemes like the Leeds–Liverpool and Bradford Canals; both Piece Halls and the Worsted Committee, all began their life here.

The Toll Booth and the Hall of Pleas, Ivegate, c. 1800. These buildings were at the opposite end of Ivegate's steep hill. The ancient manorial courts (Baron and Leet) were held in the tall structure to the left of this painting, which also housed the old town dungeon where John Nelson, the early Methodist, was imprisoned in 1744 because of his religious beliefs.

Octagon Chapel, Horton Road. Despite Nelson's experiences John Wesley was better received in Bradford, where Methodism was permanently accepted by 1756. After a temporary home at the old Cock Pit, Turls Green, a new chapel was built by subscription on a site just above the old Alexandra Hotel in Great Horton Road (1776). The octagonal shape was ideal for preaching and worship and soon attracted a large congregation. By 1810 the building was structurally unsound and not spacious enough for the large Bradford circuit and was consequently demolished.

Peckover Street, c. 1800. Formerly known as Church Street, it used to run along the south side of a private estate which, complete with ornamental lake, belonged to the Quaker banker and industrialist Edmund Peckover. Peckover, with his nephew Charles Harris, founded Bradford's second major bank in 1803. The lower house in the centre of this painting was owned by Harris and by 1825 it had been opened as the original Bradford Dispensary. It later moved to larger premises and finally, in 1843, became the Bradford Infirmary in Lumb Lane.

Bermondsey, *c.* 1835. In the first half of the nineteenth century this was one of the busiest thoroughfares in the town. Running parallel to Cheapside it dropped down sharply to what is now Forster Square. It was made up principally of wool warehouses like the one in the centre of Crichton's painting, easily spotted by the vertical row of loading doors from the upper storey. Much of Bermondsey was demolished in 1882 to make way for the Midland Station and Hotel.

A photograph of the same area prior to demolition in 1882.

Manor Hall, Kirkgate. These two pictures trace the sad demise of Bradford's principal residence during the nineteenth century. It had been built in 1705 by the lords of the manor, the Rawson family, on a site later occupied by the Kirkgate Market (now Arndale Centre). In the bottom picture the Hall's orchards and landscaped gardens have been overrun by market traders and costermongers of the Bradford Green Market, and the building itself had become a Temperance Hotel.

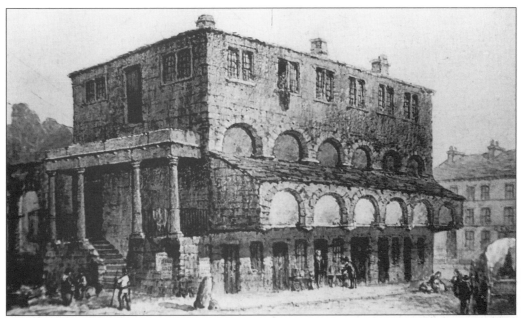

Old Market Hall, 1790. Part of this building in New Street (later Market Street) was erected by private funds in 1782. It was later (1801) completed at the expense of the lord of the manor, Benjamin Rawson, who brought back the idea for its design from his travels in Italy. It never found favour with the people and traders of Bradford and there were few tears shed when it became necessary to pull it down in 1825 to make way for the Exchange Building.

The Old Butter Market, Darley Street, c. 1830. Originally the ground floor of the Toll Booth (in Ivegate) had served as a butter market, but in 1824 the lord of the manor completely replanned the town's market facilities and erected this building behind the Manor Hall as a butter market. It was eventually demolished to make way for the Kirkgate Market in 1866.

Old Bank, Kirkgate, 1880. Built in 1813, this used to form part of the Bradford Banking Company but, in 1870, it was acquired by Beckett and Co. with Mr J.H. Lincely as manager.

Broadstones, c. 1800. This narrow street was one of the quietest parts of pre-industrial Bradford. It was located close to the ancient Church Bridge, one of several crossing points of the Bradford Beck. The narrow alleys of Broadstones could be found between the end of Kirkgate and the land dropping away from the Parish Church (modern Forster Square). On low ground, at the end of the confluence of several becks, Broadstones was liable to flooding and in 1837 torrential rain filled both Thornton and Bowling Becks putting the whole area under six feet of water causing loss of life.

Two

Highways and Byways

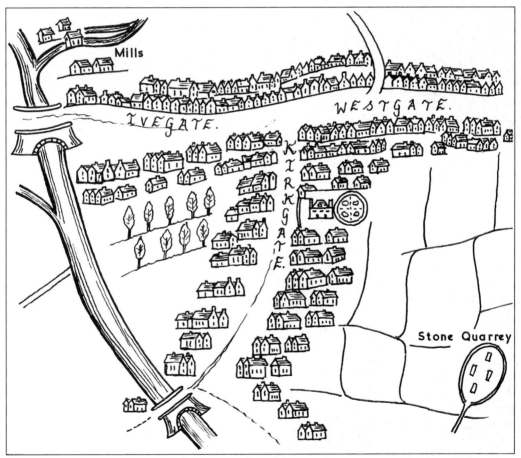

A map of Old Bradford, 1722. This is an enlarged extract from a surveyor's plan of Horton in 1722 which, for all its weaknesses, does give a clear view of Bradford before the onset of urbanisation and industrialisation. The township continues to be arranged around its compact medieval streets of Kirkgate, Ivegate and Westgate; coming together within the bend of the Bradford Beck. It shows Church Bridge (leading to the Parish Church) and Ive Bridge (leading to Goodmansend and Bowling Lane). The original market cross was situated at the junction of the three streets, and Kirkgate is dominated by the Manor Hall and its orchards.

Kirkgate, 1879. The principal highways of Bradford had changed drastically by 1850. Here, the original premises of the Bradford Banking Company occupy the corner site of the junction of Kirkgate with Darley Street. Directly opposite can be seen the gilt statue of a hound (behind the lampost) over the main entrance of the Talbot Hotel.

Talbot Hotel, Kirkgate, 1880. Since the previous century the hotel had been the unofficial headquarters of the Bradford Tories. After 1832, Bradford 'blues' such as Frank Duffield and George Banks celebrated election victories from the upper windows.

Ivegate, 1860. By 1850 Ivegate's status as a main Bradford thoroughfare had deteriorated. Shops and retailers ignored it because of its steepness and its narrow corridors. The Roebuck Inn was the unionist headquarters during the great Bradford strike of 1825.

Westgate, 1893. Taken from the junction with Ivegate and Kirkgate. The street is dominated by the Central Hotel (formerly Temperance) and Lingards new shopping emporium (with flagpole).

Darley Street, c. 1930. Originally this was part of the lord of the manor's forty acres of demesne land adjoining the manor Hall. It is thought to have been named after Darley Hall, the family home of the lords of the manor. By the time of this photograph Darley Street had a reputation for being the city's most fashionable street. To the centre of the photograph is an entrance to Kirkgate Market. This photograph was taken from a position at the bottom of Darley Street looking towards North Parade.

Town Hall Square, 1910. This photograph gives us a distinct flavour of city life prior to the First World War. A busy Tyrrel Street provides the backcloth to the square, which was a terminus for several trams, including this one to Queensbury. The queue for the tram was housed in these specially provided wooden stations.

Forster Square, c. 1910. Yet another terminus for the public transport system in the town, this one overlooked by the tower of the parish church and the impressive façade of the Post Office. The centre of the square is dominated by the imposing bronze statue of the Yorkshire 'Factory King', Richard Oastler, which was unveiled in 1869 by the seventh Earl of Shaftsbury. The figures of the small factory children moved Margaret McMillan to tears on her first visit to Bradford as she emerged from the railway station opposite.

Victoria Square, 1920. Another important Bradford square, this was located at the junction of Manchester Road and Little Horton Lane. The square is dominated by a bronze statue of Queen Victoria, twelve feet high and weighing three tons. the sculptor was Alfred Drury and the plinth and surround were designed by J.W. Simpson, architect of the Cartwright Hall. Dressed in the regalia of her Golden Jubilee of 1887, the Queen looks towards the Town Hall over a truly Victorian city.

Town Hall Square, 1920. A view looking across the Square from Tyrrel Street towards Chapel Lane. The Unitarian Chapel (extreme right) had been re-sited here in 1869. Adjoining the chapel are the premises of S. Dalby, fine art dealer and, later this century, H.J. Knutton, sports outfitters. On the left of the photograph is part of the Town Hall built in 1873 following a design competition won by the Bradford architects, Lockwood and Mawson. Here, in one picture, is a time-line of transport change: horse and cart, electric tram, and motor car.

Manningham Lane, *c.* 1895. Looking westwards out of the city, in the direction of Keighley and Skipton, this road had become a principal Bradford highway following the opening of Lister Park in 1870. Twenty-seven years later the retailing potential of this new precinct was realised with the erection of the Royal Arcade (seen here with flag pole and Gothic tower), better-known to most Bradfordians as 'Busby's'. Originally, the building was conceived as a parade of individual shops with living accommodation above, but in 1908 the well-known Kirkgate retailer Ernest W. Busby moved in to occupy most of the premises.

Manningham Lane, 1895, this time looking towards the centre of the town and the junction with North Parade (newly created as a result of the extension of Darley Street in 1879). The Yorkshire Penny Bank built in 1895 dominates the centre of the photograph. On the right, shoppers bypass the Royal Arcade, and across the road is the Theatre Tavern.

Peel Square, *c.* 1890. Robert Peel's statue was an expression of gratitude from Bradford's men of commerce for Peel's free trade policy. Surrounded by the profusely carved warehouses of Charles Street, Hall Ings, and Leeds Road, the statue was unveiled in 1855 in the presence of its sculptor, William Behnes. Since 1957, the statue has been located in Peel Park.

Manchester Road, 1901. At the junction with Mayo Avenue, this main highway in and out of the city looks like a mud-churned street of the American West, amply littered with piles of horse dung. Horse-drawn transport was still very much the order of the day at the end of the Victorian era.

Town Hall Square, *c.* 1904. The style of this fine Town Hall is essentially Gothic Revival, using architectural detail developed in the middle of the thirteenth century. Although Gothic in style, the 200-ft clock tower is copied from the original campanile of the Palazzo Vecchio in Florence. The stone used for the original building (a large extension was added to the rear of the building in 1909) was Gaisby Rock, taken from the Cliffe Wood Quarries in Bolton Road. Here, as the tram enters Market Street, bunting still adorns the premises of A. Ogden & Son, at the bottom of Manchester Road (perhaps a photograph taken shortly after the royal visit of 1904?).

Tyrrel Street. Two views of this fashionable and busy inner-city highway (now demolished) prior to the outbreak of war in 1914. For almost ninety years, until its closure in 1969, Collinson's Café (above) was a 'haven of fragrant elegance for city shoppers' and, if the wind was in the right direction, even passers-by could catch the aroma of freshly-ground coffee from one of its 22 different flavours of roasted coffee. Moreover, a three-piece orchestra played on a balcony outside the smoke room where wool men gathered to discuss trade and do deals. Below: the busy junction of Tyrrel Street with Bridge Street and Sunbridge Road.

Tyrrel Street, 1891. The same junction twenty years earlier, looking towards Bank Street and Hustlergate. To the left are the impressive premises of George Thorpe, the town's most successful drapery business, and across the road the recently-built (1871) emporium of Brown & Muff. In the centre are the premises of the Bradford Commercial Bank (1868) in Hustlergate. This is very much a businessmen's street; there are not many women here.

Toller Lane, 1900. An open-top tram rattles its ungainly way into the leafy suburb of Manningham on the No. 49 route (Duckworth Lane/Sunbridge Road).

Paper Hall, Barkerend Road, 1892. Beyond Church Bank, High Street ran into Barkerend Road which, in turn, led to the Otley Road, an old coaching highway. Here, Barkerend is in the process of being drawn into the city's urban sprawl of the late nineteenth century. The tall gabled building to the right is the ancient Paper Hall. This fine yeoman's residence (the origin of its name has never been satisfactorily confirmed) had already lost much of its splendour by 1750 and in 1794 part of the premises was tenanted by James Garnett, manufacturer, who installed hand-driven spinning machines (mules), employing a dozen operatives. Does this make it Bradford's first spinning factory?

Work People's Housing, 1920. As early as 1854 the newly-formed Bradford Corporation sought to prohibit the building of back-to-back houses but the large numbers of immigrants pouring into the prosperous wool town after 1840 meant that there was little prospect of the success of such bye-laws – back-to-back housing was the easiest solution to the city's housing problem. As late as 1921 Bradford still had 41,000 such houses (54.4% of the total housing stock) and 3,700 of them were unfit for human habitation. The post-1918 demand for accommodation ensured that most of them continued to be lived in. Only after the Second World War was a programme of standardised municipal housing commenced.

Hannah Gate, Bowling Lane. These back-to-back cottages built around an open square of communal ashpits and privies had been constructed in the 1840s between Ashley Street and Lumby Street but they were ready for demolition when this photograph was taken in 1937.

Lapage Street, 1908. Bettter-quality housing was available for the artisan class, like these solid terraced houses built in the suburbs of Laisterdyke and Manningham during the 1890s. It was in one such house – 5 Saltburn Place, Manningham – that the young J.B. Priestley was raised. This is Lapage Street looking towards the gas works in Bowling Back Lane.

Hunt Yard, 1965. This old thoroughfare, off Great Horton Road, was demolished in the late 1960s to make way for sheltered accommodation for the elderly. The origin of its name lies in Bradford's medieval history, when Bradfordale was one large forest. In the Cliffe Wood (Peel Park) area of the forest a boar roamed wild, causing much damage and fear. The Lord of the Manor promised a reward to anyone who could kill the boar. John Northrop of Bolton did so with his bow and arrow as the boar drank from a well. He cut out its tongue as proof and set off to the Manor Court to claim reward. Someone else later found the dead carcase, cut off its head and hurried to the Court also. Just as he was claiming the reward, Northrop arrived and

produced the boar's tongue to prove it was he who had killed the boar. For his reward, the Lord of the Manor gave him the piece of land on which Hunt Yard stands today; and this piece of Bradford's history now forms the basis of the city's armorial bearings and coat of arms.

Goitside, 1980, another vestige of Bradford's medieval history. The word 'goyt' means mill race, and beneath this paved road can be found the old Bradford Beck, which had provided the power to drive the manorial corn mill (modern Millergate). Most of the town's ancient watercourse had been covered by the mid-nineteenth century but not before this area (looking towards Silsbridge Lane) had become one of Bradford's most notorious ghettoes. In the 1850s it was densely over-populated by Irish immigrants, who had their own language and culture distinguishing them from the rest of Bradford's urban population.

Three
Special Events

Bradford Moor Barracks. It was here that a company of the 5th Dragoon Guards was stationed throughout the 1840s when physical force Chartism was at its height in Bradford and when social revolution threatened. In the half century after 1884 the Barracks were occupied successfully by the Green Howards, 70th West Riding Brigade Royal Artillery and the Royal Army Service Corps.

THE FIRST NATIONAL COUNCIL OF THE I.L.P.
Back Row (left to right)—A. Field, J. Kennedy, J. Lister (Treasurer).
Centre Row (left to right)—G. S. Christie, J. W. Buttery, Joseph Burgess, W. H. Drew, L. Aveling, Alf. Settle,
W. Johnson, W. Small, Chisholm Robertson, George Carson.
Seated (left to right)—Pete Curran, Shaw Maxwell (Secretary), K. St. John Conway.

Independent Labour Party, 1893. Following the failure of working-class Chartist riots in the 1840s, the labour movement channelled its energies into more democratic methods and with the success of the Bradford Labour Union in the general election of 1892 (i.e. independent of the Liberal Party), Bradford was chosen as the venue of the inaugural conference of the Independent Labour Party in 1893. In this photograph the newly-elected National Council stands before the Labour Institute (formerly a chapel in Peckover Street). Some fiery socialists attended that first conference: Keir Hardie, George Bernard Shaw, Robert Blatchford, and Fred Jowett.

Socialist Sunday School outing, c. 1925. It was Fred Jowett who had formed the Bradford Labour Church in 1891, presenting the moral gospel of socialism. The Socialist Sunday Schools were a natural extension of the I.L.P. as a cultural and social movement. They aimed at educating children in the moral virtues of socialism but the I.L.P. also provided an infrastructure of leisure and entertainment with its rambles, cycling clubs, and dramatic societies. Here a young Vic Feather stands on the East Bradford Social Sunday School processional cart as it is about to leave for the traditional May Day parade through the city.

34

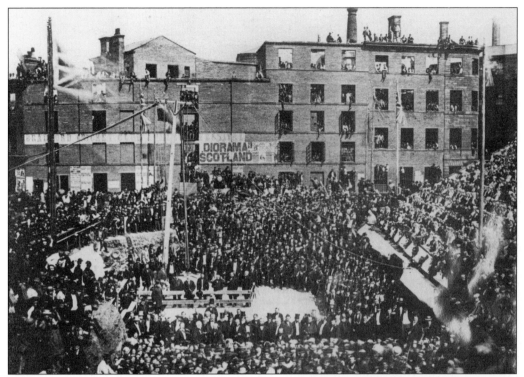

Laying the foundation stone of Bradford's Town Hall, 1870. In 1867, Bradford Corporation's Financial and General Purposes Committee agreed to accept the tender of John Ives & Son of Shipley for the building of new municipal offices on the Old Foundry site in the centre of Bradford. Amid great ceremony, the foundation stone was laid by the Mayor, Alderman Mark Dawson, on 16 May 1870.

Woodburytype.

MARK DAWSON,

MAYOR OF BRADFORD,

Nov. 1869 to Nov. 1871.

Appleton & Co., Bradford.

Mark Dawson, Mayor of Bradford, 1869–1871. Following a controversial election to the Mayoral Chair in 1869, Mark Dawson worked assiduously for his adopted town. He had been born in Manchester in 1819 and had come to Bradford in 1848. He lived at Lightcliffe and was Councillor for the East Ward from 1863. It was he who proposed the Council's purchase of Lister Park in October 1870. He also served the town as its Chief Magistrate.

Jubilee Bonfire, 1897. This enormous pile at Reevy Beacon was the City of Bradford's Municipal Jubilee bonfire. Queen Victoria's Diamond Jubilee coincided with the golden jubilee of Bradford's municipal status. The council, mindful of the town's phenomenal growth in the intervening years, petitioned the Queen to raise Bradford to the rank of a city. Thus, these men and boys of Great Horton had cause to enjoy a double celebration in that summer of 1897.

Coronation Celebrations, Norwood Green, 1902. The Victorian age ended on 22 January 1901 with the death of the old Queen. Owing to his illness King Edward's coronation was postponed until the summer of 1902. Norwood Green's coronation celebrations took place on Saturday 9 August of that year, when a procession of school-children and the Parish Council was accompanied to Field Head Farm by the Brighouse and Raistrick Temperance Brass Band. The children of the village enjoyed side-shows and rides on two decorated motor cars. They were given coronation mugs followed by an enormous bunfight at the school. In the evening their parents roasted a sheep and toasted the health of the new King. The Edwardian era had begune.

Little Horton Lane, 1904. Wednesday 4 May 1904 will long be a day to remember in the annals of Bradford with the visit of the new king's eldest son (later King George V) and his wife, Princess Mary. They were in Bradford to open the Bradford Exhibition at Cartwright Hall, Lister Park (opened by Lord Masham only a month before). Tens of thousands of Bradfordians turned out to welcome the Royal couple in fine spring weather. Here, at the junction of Little Horton Lane and the bottom of Manchester Road, the crowd was at its heaviest with every balcony, window sill and rooftop occupied.

The Victoria Statue, Little Horton Lane, 1904. Later that same day and following the visit to the Exhibition, the royal couple returned to Bradford centre for the unveiling of Queen Victoria's statue. A wooden gallery was specially erected for the occasion and 3,000 Bradford schoolchildren sang for the royal guests. Here, the great lady's grandson officially unveils the statue before a crowd of 70,000 people and with the backdrop of the Horton Lane Congregational Chapel. Brilliant sunshine, the pomp and ceremony of military bands, the colour and style of thousands of ladies' hats, all made it a day to remember.

Bradford Exhibition, 1904. This is one of the great events in Bradford's long history. The exhibition was opened in Lister Park on 4 May 1904 by the Prince and Princess of Wales using a golden key. The exhibition coincided with some warm sunny weather and when it closed in the following November 2.5 million people had attended. In the top photograph is the main Industrial Hall, which housed an impressive range of Bradford textile goods as well as textile machinery. Below is the water chute, one of several popular attractions for the masses which also included a crystal maze, gravity railway, and captive balloon.

Somali Village, Bradford Exhibition, 1904. In what was patronisingly called 'the Women's Section', the exhibition included displays on education, domestic science, and arts and crafts. One of the most popular sites of the section was a reconstruction of a real Somali village inhabited by natives of that country for the duration of the event. For months they were a continuous public spectacle. Several of their huts burned down and a number of them died here of influenza (it is said they are buried in Scholemoor Cemetery).

Eastbrook Hall, *c.* 1910. Here male Methodists spill out of Eastbrook Hall into Leeds Road at the end of an Eastbrook Brotherhood meeting. The Brotherhood became a model for men's Methodist meetings everywhere after its foundation by Revd H.M. Nield in September 1904. Nield and his successor, Revd G.G. Muir, attracted many celebrated speakers to the meetings including A. Conan Doyle, the Lord Bishop of Bradford, and Gypsy Smith. In the lower photograph the Labour MP Arthur Henderson, former iron moulder and trade unionist, prepares to address the Brotherhood in 1920.

Belle Vue Barracks, Manningham Lane, 1914. As Europe slithered and slipped towards war the 16th Battalion, Prince of Wales' Own West Yorkshire Regiment, was mobilised. Four days later 1,000 men responded to the call to arms to form E365, assembling here at Belle Vue Barracks. In this photograph, outside the Barracks and adjoining Belle Vue Hotel, news breaks of the declaration of war.

Midland Railway Yard, 1914. Bradford was one of the first towns to form its own Citizens' Army League of volunteers for the war. In September, Field Marshal Kitchener approved this Bradford battalion, later to be known as the 'Bradford Pals'. With their headquarters at the skating rink in Manningham Lane, they drilled in local parks with obsolete Lee Enfield rifles. Later that year they trained at Skipton and Ripon. Here, the battalion prepares to leave Bradford for Liverpool Docks bound for Marseilles via Egypt and, ultimately, for The Somme.

Newlands Mill disaster, 1882. Until the more recent fire disaster at Bradford City's football ground, this was the town's worst tragedy. It happened on a site between Ripley Street and Upper Castle Street, off Manchester Road. For some days before the collapse of the mill chimney there had been fears that it was in danger of falling. They were sadly realised just after 9.00am on 28 December 1882. Most of the mill workers had just settled down to their breakfast. In the week following, 53 bodies were recovered from the huge pile of devastation seen here. Many of those killed were teenage mill girls, whose parents had great difficulty identifying them.

Tram Crash 1907. There were only two fatalities in the history of the Bradford trams. Surprisingly it did not include this dramatic accident of 31 July 1907 when car 210, returning from Undercliffe into the city, gathered speed in Barkerend Road and hurtled out of control down Church Bank. As it was 6 a.m. there were few passengers aboard but thirteen people were injured as the top deck was smashed and the tram hit a warehouse and overturned.

Four
Public Buildings

Post Office Building, c. 1900. Despite the intrusion of the Oastler monument to the right and the tower of the parish church looming through the mist to the left, this photograph, taken at the turn of the century, is dominated by the General Post Office building in Forster Square. This first opened for business on 1 September 1887, replacing an old buildng in Union Passage (Bank Street). It was designed by Sir Henry Tanner and its construction led to the demolition of that warren of alleys, courts, and yards known as Broadstones. It is a fine symmetrical Victorian structure, but somewhat obsolete to the Bradford of the 1990s.

Parish Church, 1900. Of all Bradford's public buildings, this is the most enduring. It is the third church to have been built on this site. The first is said to have dated from the seventh century, and a later church, built in 1200 A.D., was destroyed by the Scots almost a century later. It became a cathedral in 1919, by which time it had succumbed completely to urban sprawl and to its own graveyard. The road to the right is Church Bank, leading to Barkerend Road (High Street).

Old Court House, Hall Ings. In the first half of the nineteenth century, Bradford produced several public buildings in the neo-classical style, but this was by far the purest. It consisted of three storeys with a front elevation of seven bays; the central three forming a portico, the pediment of which was supported by four Ionic columns. It was built in 1834 and cost the Bradford public £7,000. This photograph was taken just after the Second World War and by 1958 the building had been controversially demolished.

St George's Hall, Hall Ings & Bridge Street, 1910. In 1849, Bradford's highly-principled city fathers ordered an inquiry into the town's declining moral condition. This building was one of their solutions to the lower-class preference for the numerous brothels and singing rooms attached to the town's public houses. Built in 1852 to a design by Bradford architects Lockwood & Mawson, it was officially opened on 31 August 1853 under the patronage of Queen Victoria and Prince Albert and the presidency of the Earl of Harewood. It quickly established a reputation as a concert hall for choral and orchestral music attracting many famous Victorian artistes and speakers like Jenny Lind, Charles Hallé, and Mrs Sunderland. The hall could seat 4,000 people and the quality of its acoustics encouraged the formation of the Bradford Festival Choral Society in 1858. Apart from the years 1923–48, when it was used as a cinema, this magnificent concert hall continues to be the city's main cultural and musical forum.

The Salt Statue, 1888. This statue had pride of place in front of the new town hall until it became a nuisance to traffic flow in 1896. It was erected in Salt's lifetime (1874) as a tribute to his commercial and public service to Bradford. Everyone subscribed to the public statue, even individual children contributed their pennies. Suitably modest, Salt resisted the decision to erect such a monument, declaring, 'You are going to turn me into a pillar of Salt'. There was no cause for modesty, for he had been the second Mayor of the town, and President of the Bradford Chamber of Commerce. In 1859 he was elected Member of Parliament for Bradford; he also served as a magistrate, later becoming the Deputy Lieutenant for the West Riding. A public holiday was declared when the statue was unveiled by the Duke of Devonshire in 1874. It was later moved to Lister Park, where it can be found today, close to the Norman Arch entrance to the park.

Telegraph and Argus Building, Drake Street. For many years, this building has served as the home of the city's principal newspaper, *The Telegraph and Argus*, but in 1853, when it was opened, it was erected as a home trade warehouse for the highly successful business partnership of Robert Milligan and Henry Forbes, who purchased a site alongside that of the St George's Hall, and adjoining on the other side the Court House (recently erected in Greek Revival style). The architects, Andrews and Delaunay, modelled this warehouse on the merchant palaces of medieval Florence. With each storey clearly delineated by means of firm wall mouldings and window balconies, the façade is topped by a projecting cornice. This, according to John Roberts, became a standard pattern for Bradford's commercial buildings up to 1875.

Mechanics Institute, Tyrrel Street, 1890. Certainly the pattern is continued here with the new Mechanics Institute building opened in 1871 on a site adjoining Market Street, Tyrrel Street, and Bridge Street. Founded in 1852 as an adult education centre, the Institute had thrived in premises in Piccadilly and Well Street. Such was the demand for artisan education that even larger premises were required by 1870. Bradford's captains of industry like Ripley, Salt, and Isaac Holden donated generously, and this fine Italianate building (designed by Andrews and Pepper) was the result. This excellent building was demolished in the 1970s.

Manningham Mills, Lilycroft Road, *c.* 1920. Technically not a public building, this is nevertheless a landmark in the cityscape. This huge and imposing structure was erected in 1872/3 by Samuel Cunliffe Lister (later Lord Masham) to replace an earlier mill destroyed by fire. These two blocks of six storeys have a frontage of 350 yards in Heaton Road. Here, Silk Street gives a clear clue to the origin of Lister's wealth and commerce. Using silk waste, Listers of Manningham became famous for their weaving of silk velvet. It was the ancestors of these children, in these streets, who had taken strike action against a wage reduction in 1891 and precipitated the move towards an Independent Labour Party.

Old Infirmary, Westgate, *c.* 1900. This is the dispensary entrance to the Old Infirmary in Westgate. The dispensary itself was opened in 1873 but the main building of the Infirmary was opened for in-patients in 1843 and was considerably extended twenty years later. The mock-Tudor style of the original building was followed in all subsequent extensions, including a new wing in 1885. Twelve years later, Queen Victoria gave permission for the hospital to be named the Bradford Royal Infirmary.

Wool Exchange, Market Street, 1960. The Bradford Exchange was a commercial institution with a worldwide reputation. It was built at a cost of £40,000 and the foundation stone was laid by Lord Palmerston in 1864. Its Gothic exterior is dominated by a pinnacled clock tower over the main entrance. Inside is an impressive hammer-beam roof. A fine statue of Richard Cobden, the godfather of free trade in the nineteenth century, occupies a prominent position in the central assembly room where members of the Exchange gathered to buy and sell wool.

At one time the Wool Exchange had over three thousand subscribers representing many countries of the world. Although colonial wool from Australasia and South Africa was the main source of supply there were imports from Turkey, China, Peru, Tibet, and the East Indies, in addition to the home wools from Lincolnshire, Leicestershire, and Kent. Market days were usually Mondays and Thursdays and here, in 1905, there is a good attendance by all of the town's leading firms and businesses.

Bradford Free Library, Darley Street. A reference library and reading rooms were first opened in 1872 when the council voted to adopt the recently passed Free Libraries Act. Rooms were taken in Market Street, and Alderman Samuel Smith sold 13,400 volumes of his private collection of books to the council. In the following year a lending department run by Charles Virgo attracted a wide cross section of the Bradford public. An early borrowers list included a comedian, a barrister, four cloggers, sixteen erand boys, three barmaids, two auctioneers, 95 overlookers, 143 schoolboys, 400 clerks, and 582 warehousemen. In due course the library moved to these premises in Darley Street where an art gallery and public museum were added.

Victoria Hotel, Bridge Street, 1971. Built in 1867 directly facing the Exchange Railway Station, this hotel was constructed specifically for the new railway age. It was designed by Bradford's leading architects of the time, Francis Lockwood and William Mawson. It was originally known as the Great Northern Hotel.

Kirkgate Market, 1895. Bradford's right to hold a market had been granted by Henry III in 1251. In 1866 the rights were acquired by the council from the lord of the manor and by 1871 the council had built this imposing structure designed by the ubiquitous Lockwood and

Mawson. It was opened on 31 October 1872, and a wide range of goods was sold from interior and exterior shops and stalls, well patronised and now remembered for their friendly service and homely atmosphere. On the corner, at the junction with Darley Street, can be seen Leuchter's Restaurant, famous for hosting the oyster supper in April 1890 at which the Barbarians Rugby Club was formed.

Kirkgate Market, Godwin Street, 1970. Perhaps the least memorable of Kirkgate Market's three entrances, all of which displayed some impressive carvings above their archways. Over the Kirkgate entrance (No. 80) were the sculpted figures of Flora and Pomona, the goddesses of flowers and fruit; subsequent to the demolition of the market this stonework was retained at the Bradford Industrial Museum. With the ironwork on the roof beyond repair, this popular and comfortable market place had to go and in 1973, despite a petition signed by 25,000 Bradfordians urging its retention, the whole site was flattened for redevelopment. The author is but one who regrets its passing.

Bowling Green Hotel, Bridge Street, *c.* 1870. A fine example of an old English hostelry, one of the most popular coaching inns of the town. Its large open frontage, balcony and bays also made it the ideal electioneering headquarters for the town's Whigs/Liberals. By 1870 its central position was ripe for redevelopment and it gave way graciously to the Mechanics Institute building.

White Swan Inn, *c.* 1830. Another old inn to concede to Bradford's mid-Victorian urban development programme was the White Swan at the junction of Charles Street and Market Street. In the old coaching days this inn was the staging post for the 'Highflyer' coach. In 1878 Angus Holden (then mayor of Bradford) and several other businessmen commissioned architects Milnes and France to design a new concept in urban retailing – the Swan shopping arcade – on the site of the old inn.

Swan Arcade. This four-storeyed building (plus an attic storey) originally provided for 46 offices on the upper floors and 44 shops at ground-floor level. There were also 65 market rooms for the wool trade and it was in one of these that the very young J.B. Priestley began his working career as a junior clerk with Helm & Company. He later wrote that 'Swan Arcade was no ordinary roofed-over huddle of gift shops: it was on the grand scale.' Priestley fought a vigorous campaign to prevent its demolition and closure in 1962 and he never quite forgave Bradford for an act of self-mutilation when it was replaced by Arndale House in 1964. There were entrances from three streets and here can be seen the one used by young Priestley, from Market Street, with an oriel window above.

Swan Arcade interior, 1961. In the early days the imposing archways and ironwork gates led many to think it was private property. A feature of Swan Arcade was its mirrors. The names of ground-floor retailers were originally painted on the windows against a background which kept out the light. Consequently, mirrors specially imported from Paris were installed so that they reflected light from outside and into the shops and offices. Later, there were mirrors inside the arcade angled downwards from the sides of the avenues. Here can be seen a fine balance of glass, ironwork, and carved stonework – perhaps Priestley was right.

Front right are the banking premises of Bechet & Co., a Leeds bank (1758) which had opened a branch here in 1833. Above, and on the same side of the road is the old Post Office and the premises of the Bradford Banking Co. On the other side of the road, the 'hound' of the Talbot Hotel can just be discerned.

Wilson's Restaurant, Kirkgate, 1920. Wilsons were originally corn dealers in the town but by 1900 had become noted for their confectionery and restaurant. These ancient bow-fronted premises were demolished in 1920 to make way for the Anglo-South American Bank, which was a British institution founded in 1889 to encourage the nitrate trade with Chile. After 1918, Bradford spinners requiring raw wool were increasingly turning to the Argentine Republic, Uruguay, and South Brazil for their supplies and to Peru and Bolivia for alpaca wool, hence the opening of this new branch of the bank.

Cartwright Hall, 1960. Situated in Bradford's most popular park, Lister Park, the hall was built on the site of Lord Masham's first family home. He gave £47,000 for its erection as a permanent monument to the pioneering inventor of the power loom and wool combine machine, Dr Edmund Cartwright. It was officially opened by Lord Masham (S.C. Lister of Manningham Mills) on 13 April 1904. The Italianate design is that of J.W. Simpson; the stone was quarried from Bolton Woods, and the grounds laid out as an Italian garden with bandstand and spacious promenades. The foundation stone was laid in 1900 but it took four years to build. Until recent years it has served as the city's central musuem and art gallery as well as a botanical gardens. Do you remember the bees?

Midland Hotel, Forster Square. When opened in March 1890 the Midland Station and Hotel ranked as one of the leading railway centres in the country. The scheme had first been mooted as early as 1874 but railway revenues would not permit the immediate construction of such an ambitious project. It took five years to build and cost over a million pounds. The station had six platforms and was directly linked to the sixty-room hotel whose main public entrance was in Kirkgate. Standing in Forster Square the photographer looks back towards Kirkgate with Cheapside off to the right.

Five

Between the Wars

Market Street, *c.* 1920. After the 1914–18 war, Bradford's wool textile industry had its ups and downs as a result of domestic contraction, world economic recession and overseas tariff barriers. One pessimist commented that 'grass would grow in the streets of Bradford', but he was a false prophet and the town and its industry weathered the storm to compete in new markets, adapt to new technology, and make new profits (albeit not of the scale of the nineteenth century). Here, Market Street looks as busy and as provincially prosperous as it ever had in Victorian times. However, appearances can be deceptive, for between 1928 and 1932 almost four hundred Bradford textile firms went out of business and those unemployed in Bradford reached 35,000 in 1931.

Say 'No' to Bradford, 1937. During the nineteenth century, Bradford's municipal boundaries expanded to include Bolton (1873), Allerton and Heaton (1882), Eccleshill, Idle Bierley, Tong, Thornton and Wyke (1889) and Clayton in 1930. Several attempts by Bradford to include Shipley have been vigorously and successfully resisted. The last, in 1937, was rejected by the House of Lords and provoked a massive popular outcry. Here, a public protest reaches its climax outside Shipley's new town hall (1932) with a protest march led by the Salts Prize Band and Fire Brigade.

Little Germany, c. 1939. This rooftop view overlooks the unique warehousing area of Little Germany between the wars. From these buildings the city's merchant princes had continued to contribute to the town's economy after 1918. From these warehouses in Peckover Street and Barkerend Road, overseas sales of finished cloth were in decline as traditional markets in the USA and Western Europe gradually closed. To compensate, the merchants in these premises established new markets in the Far East and Eastern Europe, particularly China and Poland. As a consequence, the industry's (and Bradford's) inter-war export record was not as bad as it might have been. Through the smog, in the middle distance, you can just pick out the heavy arched roof of the Exchange railway station.

Bradford Dyers Association, Well Street, c. 1950. The B.D.A. was once the largest commission dyeing and finishing company in the world. It had been formed in 1898 when a number of master dyers combined to fix their prices in the face of falling profits and overseas competition. Between the wars, the B.D.A. moved into these premises at 39 Well Street. Here (top photograph far right) the main entrance, at the bottom of Church Bank, precedes a magnificent façade of five storeys of round headed windows. It had originally been built as a wool warehouse in 1867. Exactly a century later, the premises were bought by the Carrington Vyella textile group and later housed Pennine Radio. Below: the busy post-war thoroughfare of Well Street compares with the 'cul-de-sac' nature of today's street. In this photograph the view is from the Leeds Road end of Well Street looking towards Forster Square.

Forster Square. Two views of Forster Square after 1945. Prior to the construction of the Bridge Street Interchange this was Bradford's busiest transport terminal. To the extreme right is the railway station and Midland Hotel. The centre block (advertising Heys Gold Cup Ale) is part of Market Street leading to Hustlergate. The shops at the end of that block included Lavell's confectioners, Williams' storage and removals, and the Boar's Head public house. Below is a view overlooking the square from the end of Market Street. Here, queues at rush-hour await the trolleybus service to Heaton, Nab Wood and Saltaire.

Town Hall Square, *c.* 1945. The electric tram survived until after the Second World War, but by the time this photograph was taken the motorbus and trolleybus were in the ascendancy. Here are two landmarks of Bradford's post-war retailing scene, Halfords bicycle shop (left) and Burton's men's outfitters (centre).

Market Street, *c.* 1935. A busy interwar scene of Market Street and the junction with Town Hall Square, opposite the premises of the Provincial Building Society (formerly Bradford Third Equitable Benefit Building Society). The tram to Queensbury is about to pass the hosiery shop of Miss Skelton.

John Street Market, c. 1948. For nearly forty years after its opening in 1931, this glazed-roof open market between John Street and Westgate was dear to the hearts of Bradford folk regardless of social class. Built on the old site of Coppy Quarry, its 175 stalls offered ladies' lingerie, caged puppies, 'naughty' books and every conceivable boiled sweet for the children. At Dutch auctions, 'wide boys' offered give-away bargains of crockery, cheap jewellery, and household goods. To the right of this picture were several herbalists' stores which gave the market its nickname of 'Quack Market'. One character claimed he could remove eye cataracts by the use of his tongue. Who needs a National Health Service?! But it is for the aroma of hot mushy peas that the market will be best remembered. Its numerous food stalls all sold Yorkshire's second favourite alfresco dish – pie and peas.

Britannia House, Bridge Street, 1945. This 1927 building was the council's 'false start' on the inter-war central area redevelopment plan. The block was built as offices and ground-floor shops, and those old enough will remember queuing here for their wartime ration books. Its colonnaded style and intricate stonework are let down by the rather disappointing attempt at a copper dome. The building is now used as offices for the City's Finance department. The retailers O.S. Wain, on the ground floor, has been a popular rendezvous point for nervous young things of the post-war generation on their first 'date'. Well, for the author it was, anyway!

Ivegate. Two views of Ivegate between the wars. In the illustration above (*c.* 1920), the busy but quaint cobbled street is still evocative of a Bradford that has long gone. Ivegate was always well-endowed with inns and taverns, and here, at the top of the street, can be seen the Grosvenor Hotel, built upon a warren of cellars and yards famous as the scene of much criminality and immorality in the 1840s. To the left is one of several pork butchers with premises in Ivegate (many of them of German origin). In the photograph below, the motor car has brought the steep street firmly into the twentieth century. To the right is the Unicorn Hotel, which was already ancient when news reached Bradford of Wellington's success at Waterloo; and to the left are the premises of the Prudential Assurance Company, brick-built to the design of Alfred Waterhouse in 1895.

Darley Street, 1947. There have been few changes to this street scene since the photograph was taken, apart from the number and the design of cars. The building furthest from the camera is that of the furnishers Christopher Pratt & Sons in North Parade. The building with the pointed gable jutting out from the building line on the right was the Institute for the Blind (until 1962).

Manningham Lane, 1935. Here is the junction of Manningham Lane with North Parade and Manor Row. In the centre of the photograph are the premises of the Yorkshire Penny Bank, designed by J. Ledingham. The building is rich in carved decoration and is lavishly topped by the strikingly oriental clock tower.

Six
On the Move

Trams in Sunbridge Road. This double-decker tram is about to reach its terminus at the bottom of Sunbridge Road on the route from Allerton, *c.* 1920.

Shanks's Pony, *c.* 1914. While this is probably a Sunday school field day on the ouskirts of Bradford prior to the Great War it does serve to remind us that the majority of people got around their town by walking – until, that is, the arrival of the tram in the last quarter of the nineteenth century.

Laisterdyke Toll Bar, 1878. By 1800, road transport had been improved (for the movement of goods at least) by the introduction of the turnpike trusts. When this photograph was taken, the system had fallen into disuse and the ancient barhouse and gate on the Dudley Hill–Harrogate Turnpike (1736) were largely redundant. Not all Bradfordians approved of this system of road maintenance, for in 1753 there were violent scenes at several turnpike gates in Bradford Moor where gates were burnt and tollkeepers assaulted.

Spinkwell Locks, Bradford Canal, *c.* 1885. The solution to moving bulky goods like coal cheaply across the northern counties lay in the canal system which revolutionised transportation before the invention of the railways. Bradford quickly became a part of the canal network when a small Bradford canal was built in 1774 to link up with the main Leeds–Liverpool waterway at Shipley. Spinkwell Lock at Bolton was one of ten sets of locks on the three-mile stretch of the canal which could take horse-drawn barges of 61 x 14 feet (weighing 40–60 tons). The Spinkwell lock, built at the canal's highest point, was a popular picnic spot in the nineteenth century and was the last of the canal's locks to close. It was finally demolished in March 1995 to make way for industrial units and road development. The bottom picture, taken by the author in 1969, shows its derelict condition 25 years ago.

Canal Basin, Broadstones. The line of the canal ran into the very heart of the growing town in 1774, terminating at Hoppy Bridge, close to Broadstones and just below the parish church. From the outset, the owners relied upon water from the Bradford beck to fill the canal. As this became polluted with untreated sewage and was never sufficient anyway, the basin of the canal became an open sewer giving off offensive gases which occasionally caught fire. In 1845 James Smith, a government inspector, wrote that 'The water of this basin is often so charged with decaying matter that in hot weather bubbles of sulphurated hydrogen are continually rising to the surface so that watch cases and other materials of silver become black in the pockets of the workmen employed there … The stench is sometimes very strong and fevers prevail much all around … '.

Bradford Canal closure, 1922. Smith had been right, for in 1848 a cholera outbreak killed over three hundred people. Following a public outcry, a High Court injunction ruled against the owners of the canal in 1866 and a year later it was closed. When it reopened in 1871 the last quarter of a mile into the city had been filled in. The canal then began at Northbrook Bridge (seen here) with wharves in Wharf Street and Canal Street. By this time, the owners were losing business to the railways and in 1922 the canal finally closed for business and the water was drained. Here, the last barge to take cargo on the canal leaves Northbrook in the direction of Shipley in 1922.

Bradford Canal, Bolton Woods, 1955. By the middle of this century, most of the line of the canal had been filled in and only the name of the road built alongside it survived as evidence of its existence. Here, at Bolton Woods in 1955, the line of the canal can be seen as well as the remains of another set of locks (Oliver Locks) with the centre of the city in the distance.

Exchange Station 1973. After many years of trying, Bradford was finally linked to the expanding national railway network in 1846, when it joined Leeds via the Aire Valley. The Lancashire and Yorkshire Railway Company opened a line from Halifax while the Great Northern Co. provided a second link with Leeds via Bowling in 1852. Both of these required terminus stations and the Great Northern Exchange station was completerd in 1888. It was spanned by two semi-circular roof arches supported by ornamental wrought iron pillars (cf King's Cross station) and covered by plate glass. Here one of the last trains is about to leave the station for Leeds shortly before the whole site was levelled to the ground in 1973.

Horse-drawn trams, Manningham Lane, 1882. For visitors to the town in the 1880s the major change to street life was the appearance of a public transport system other than hired cabs and wagonettes. In 1882, tracks were laid from Darley Street, along Manningham Lane to the Lister Park gates. These horse-drawn street cars only went into service when their drivers deemed the number of passengers to be adequate. Here, one of the first street cars makes its leisurely way along Manningham Lane.

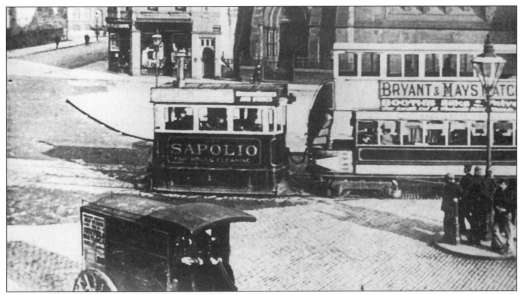

Steam Tram, Chapel Lane, *c.* 1890. The success of the new public service quickly prompted a move to steam-driven trams which were considered by some to be too noisy and too fast (12 m.p.h.) Here, a steam-driven tram passes in front of the Unitarian Chapel along Chapel Lane near Town Hall Square. The chapel was built here in 1809 and provided seating for five hundred people.

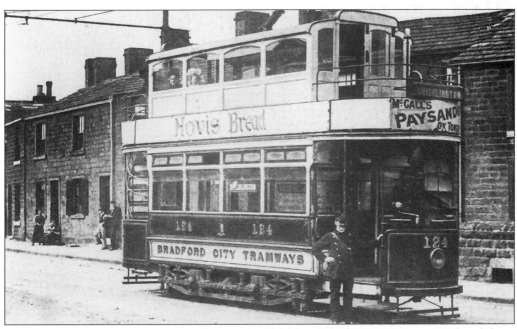

Electric Tram. The council first experimented with electrically driven trams in 1883 but did not adopt them until 1898 when a short service was run up Bolton Road. Others quickly followed, and here car 124, with fitted top, is running a service to Drighlington and back.

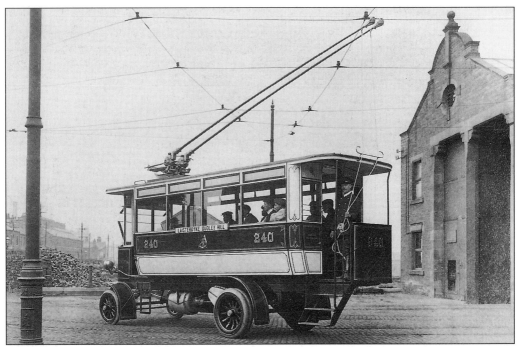

Trolley Bus, Midland Street, 1911. In 1911, Bradfordians saw the first trackless trolley bus on the streets of Bradford. Following a continental invention, Bradford was the first British municipality to adopt these galleons of the highways with their solid metal tyres. Here, car 240 is about to leave the Midland Street depot on the inaugural service between Laisterdyke and Dudley Hill. The vehicle was known as the 'Penny Joss' and the most important innovation was the driver's windscreen.

Bradford's last trolleybus in operation in 1972.

Motor buses in Forster Square. Private companies ran motor buses on the streets of Bradford as early as 1922. Three years later, the council reluctantly operated a fleet which became so popular the city's trams were doomed to extinction. Here, corporation motor buses leave and approach Forster Square on a damp dark winter afternoon in the 1950s.

Bradford's first taxi with its proud proprietor, Mr William Binns.

Traffic in Manningham Lane, 1947. The motor car became the symbol of the consumer society after 1945. When this photograph was taken there were over two million cars in use in Britain. The car has transformed this ancient Bradford highway leading out, as it does, to the commuter belt townships of Baildon, Bingley, and Ilkley. In the centre is the Theatre Royal, recently converted to a cinema, and to the right is the home of the Independent Order of Rechabites.

The introduction of the pneumatic tyre in 1880 made cycling a comfortable and popular pastime with men and women alike. In the *Post Office Directory* for Bradford in 1893 there are listed no fewer than thirteen cycling clubs, and that excludes the Clarion Cycling Club of the Independent Labour Party which was founded in Bradford in that year. Here, ladies parade their flower-adorned cycles at Great Horton Carnival in June 1905.

Seven
Schools and Schooldays

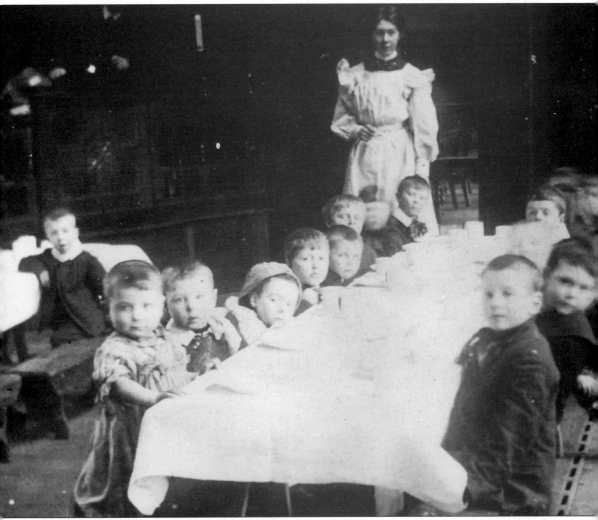

An infant class at Green Lane Board School in 1895.

Church School children, 1908. A government survey in 1844 had noted that 51 per cent of all deaths in Bradford were of children under five years of age. In 1894, Margaret Macmillan found many Bradford school-children in poor condition. 'Children with adenoids, children with curvature, children in every stage of neglect, dirt and suffering ... '. These children of the Bradford Church School on Stott Hill in 1908 were in relatively good shape although two are without footwear, one has been shaved for head lice, and their clothing has seen better days.

Lilycroft Board School, 1970. By 1870, voluntary schools like the one at Stott Hill were no longer able to provide sufficient elementary school places for Bradford's large population. In that year, W.E. Foster, M.P. for Bradford, introduced his Education Act which set up local authority provision in the shape of Board Schools. Surprisingly, Bradford required only eight new schools, one of which was this one at Lilycroft in Manningham which was designed by local architects Hope & Jardine in Gothic style. Hundreds of thousands of children have learned and played beneath its top-heavy octagonal tower, and continue to do so.

Belle Vue Higher Grade School, Manningham Lane. Bradford's School Board was highly successful in its provision of elementary education but by 1875 some children were too bright for such a basic curriculum. Equally, there were those who believed in the concept of an 'educational ladder'. As a result, schools opened in Bradford which offered more than elementary education – these were 'Higher Grade' schools and Bradford led the country with this idea. Here, the Board's second Higher Grade school was opened at Belle Vue, Manningham Lane, by W.E. Foster in 1879.

Wapping School Baths. In the years before 1914, socialists were on the move in Bradford, particularly in the field of educational welfare. Medical examinations of schoolchildren began in 1893 and the first school baths were opened shortly afterwards. Here, at Wapping in 1899, a class of young boys are given their weekly bath. A clear case of ' … next to godliness'.

Nursery Schooling. Margaret Macmillan initiated medical inspections of school chldren as early as 1893 but her suggestion that each cluster of Board Schools should have its own crèche was not received at all well and it was not until after the First World War that Bradford Council endorsed nursery education at St Ann's Roman Catholic School and later at Lilycroft and Princeville. Meals were provided and a sleep was taken every afternoon (see bottom photograph). The emphasis was on purposeful play with suitable toys, activity corners, and fresh air. Here, in the picture above, young children (2–5 years) enjoy a wide range of stimulating activities in the nursery at Princeville in 1924.

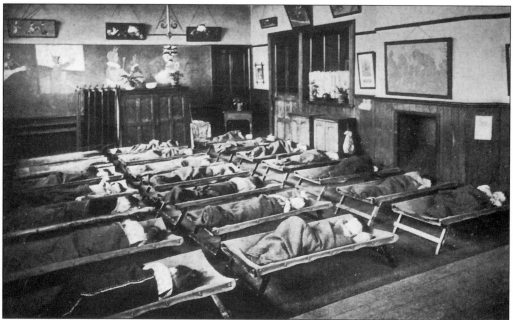

School Meals, 1908. If progress in the field of nursery education was slow in Bradford, provision of school meals was pioneering and far reaching. School meals had been given to the necessitous poor in Bradford on a voluntary basis long before the Provision of Meals Act of 1906. During 1907 a pilot scheme to provide three meals a day for forty chilren was so successful that a central cooking depot was set up at Green Lane School which cooked food for distribution to several feeding centres across the city. This photograph shows patient and hungry children at the White Abbey feeding centre in 1908. Mr Priestley, headmaster of Green Lane School, is the smaller of the two supervising teachers. In the bottom picture, eager and hungry children watch the arrival of the food in specially built motor wagons provided by the city's Tramways Committee.

School for the Blind, 1935. The earliest provision of schooling for those with eye defects was voluntary. In 1885, a group of local philanthropists led by Sir Jacob Behrens employed a Miss L. Holder to hold classes for the blind at Carlton Street School. Six children enrolled and by 1902 there were twenty-two (see top photograph). After 1915, a permanent residential school for the blind was opened as Odsal House School. By 1914, a survey across the city showed over three hundred children to be suffering from myopia. As a result, chilren like these in the bottom photograph were admitted on a daily basis to the new Daisy Hill School for Myopes (now Temple Bank School).

Physical Education, c. 1900. Under Sergeant Ryan, physical education in Bradford's early Board Schools was a crude 'drill' designed to foster discipline and obedience more than anything else. After 1888 a new curriculum was introduced with running, wrist exercises, and the use of dumb bells. Here, a class of boys is put through its paces with dumb bells, supervised by a bowler-hatted teacher!

Craftwork, 1908. After 1898, the Bradford School Board broadened the curriculum of its schools by encouraging clay modelling and woodwork. Metalwork was introduced into higher grade schools in 1899 and to all schools by 1903. Here, a woodwork class at Green Lane School is introduced to the 'plane'.

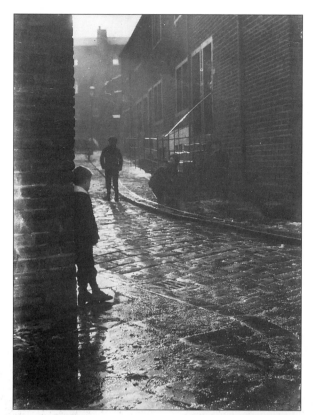

'Laikin aht', *c.* 1900. A growing appreciation among working-class parents of the benefits of a school education, the vigilance of the 'Board man', and the continuation of payment by results and attendance all contributed to Bradford's good attendance record (77 per cent in 1891; 87 per cent in 1903). As a counter to this, Bradford had the largest number of half-timers in the country and there were always children like the ones above, who preferred the freedom of the street and 'laikin aht' to the discipline of the classroom.

Standard II boys at Great Horton School in 1905.

Eight
Bradford at Work

Wool sorting office, *c.* 1900. For the greater part of the period which this book covers (1880–1950), Bradford was synonymous with wool. One writer even gave it the pseudonym of 'Worstedopolis'. Even after the inter-war depression, 38 per cent of the town's working population had jobs in textiles and 878 out of 1003 members of the Chamber of Commerce were involved in the wool trade in some way. Here, bales of raw wool arrive at the Bradford Conditioning House in Canal Road.

First Conditioning House, c. 1900. In 1891, the Chamber of Commerce had suggested some kind of testing centre for checking the moisture content and other properties of raw wool increasingly imported from colonial lands. The first premises of this valuable organisation were located behind the Town Hall, but in 1902 it was transferred to purpose-built accommodation in Cape Street, off Canal Road. This is the original building, close to the Town Hall.

The first Bradford mill. The earliest textile mills were water-powered spinning mills and consequently were located out of Bradford township where water power was never good. The first mill to be built in the town was Holme Mill on Thornton Road (below Little Horton Lane). It was built by Messrs Ramsbottom, Swaine and Murgatroyd in 1800, and was powered by a 15 h.p. steam engine. The mill was later burned down and the land sold to Richard Fawcett. This picture of the mill is an extract taken from an oil painting portrait of Fawcett and shows the four-storey building with cupola bell tower. To the rear is Horton Lane and Randall Well.

Bradford mills. The size and scale of Bradford's mills increased throughout the nineteenth century. Pictured above, the Barkerend Mill was built in 1820 for William and James Garnett. The lower photograph shows Samuel Cunliffe Lister's huge edifice at Manningham covering 16 acres of floor area and dominated by the 250-foot chimney supposedly modelled on a Venetian campanile.

Weavers at work. Although some generations apart, the women in these two photographs are both doing the time-honoured task in the local worsted trade – power loom weaving. In 1846 a survey showed that 12,000 Bradford women and girls were employed in mills. Unlike men, their work was never considered as skilled and their wages were paid accordingly. Both of these women are working in noisy, arduous, and sometimes dangerous conditions. In the top photograph, a Victorian weaver is mending a broken warp; and below, in the 1940s, a weaver fixes a pirn of weft thread into the shuttle (boat-shaped contraptions hanging from the loom).

'Mill's aht'. Of the 12,000 female mill workers in Bradford in 1846, 50 per cent were under the age of eighteen. As late as 1901 (even after legislation on child employment), 62 per cent of female workers were under the age of 25. Here, the buzzer has gone and the shift has finished. A group of carefree girls from Mount Street mill pass the off licence premises of Mr George Popplewell in Seymour Street just as a working-class woman beats a hasty, beshawled retreat with a jug of beer (?) secreted beneath her 'pinny'.

Packing Department. In 1901, 57,000 Bradfordians were employed in textiles. It is believed that in some way or other Bradford handled five sixths of this country's wool prior to the First World War and in 1910, the city's annual turnover in textiles was estimated at £90 million. Here, in the Leeds Road premises of John Shaw and Sons (Dyers), men in the packing department are hard at work.

Last Bradford Coalmine, 1938. So extensive was Bradford's worsted industry that people overlook the importance of coal mining to the town's economy and development. In 1870 there were 46 working collieries in Bradford producing almost two million tons of coal per annum. Both Bowling and Low Moor Ironworks owned and worked ten mines in the area. As Bradford is on the edge of the Yorkshire coalfield, the extensive faulting meant that supplies were inconsistent. By 1914 they were almost exhausted, so that by 1924 there were only three pits working in the area. At Thornton, a bed of fireclay was as profitable as the coal and consequently here in 1938 at the top of Thornton Road is thought to be Bradford's last coalmine. It finally closed in the early 1960s when it was operating as Brook's Thornton Fireclays, retailing under the brand name of 'Impenetra'.

Bolton Woods Quarry, c. 1910. In 1853, two working men, John Homes and Thomas Dawson, agreed with Mr Barton of Bolton Hall about the quarrying of stone at Bolton Woods. It was the beginning of a very lucrative business because the millowners of the West Riding were demanding a fine quality ashlar for their multi-storey mills and warehouses. The fine sandstone blocks from Gaisby were used in many of Bradford's public and commercial buildings, as well as those of other cities throughout Britain. In this photograph best sandstone (up to ten feet thick) is being cut by Waterhouse Denbigh & Co., subsequent owners of the quarry. There were also several stone quarries worked in the central township in the 1800s; Coppy Quarry (now John Street Market) was worked by Thackwray, Cousens and Co.

Northbrook Vitriol Works, Canal Road, 1940. Better known to Bradfordians as Leather's Chemical Co. and at one time the oldest chemical company in this country, for it had been started on this Northbrook site in 1750 by lord of the manor Benjamin Rawson. Here, the enormous lead chambers for making sulphuric acid look gloomily over the site along Canal Road. From these towers, sulphuric acid had been made since the 1870s. To the right is the Fox and Goose public house in Wharf Street.

Chemical Workers, 1895. By 1838, the Northbrook works was owned by Samuel Broadbent, whose son-in-law G.H. Leather (worsted spinner) acquired the business on Broadbent's death in 1843. At that time, acid was concentrated by boiling in open pans and the nitrous gases were allowed to go to waste in the atmosphere. Before he died in 1897, Leather had taken into partnership his nephew H.K. Burnet, grandson of Revd John Burnet, vicar of Bradford 1847–70. In this photograph, taken in 1895, the entire workforce poses before the stacks of carboys filled with acid. On the extreme left a young Tom Margerison, clerk of the company, is easily distinguished by his sartorial neatness. Sulphuric acid burned or rotted clothes easily, so these men did not appear for work in their Sunday best!

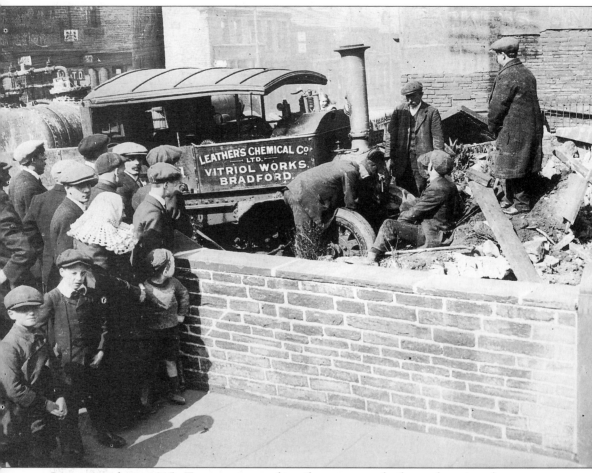

Street Accident, 1915. Transporting such a dangerous, volatile, and toxic substance was difficult, and that was probably one reason for locating the works alongside the Bradford Canal, which was immediately to the rear of the premises. Here, in June 1915, the company's steam wagon has crashed and the inquisitive onlookers show little concern for the potential hazards of a spillage. The young man standing (far right) at the scene of the crash would have cause to be wary, for seven years later he was blinded at the works when hot acid splashed into his face. His name was Nelson Sutcliffe and he subsequently became Works Manager.

Acid Chamber, 1902. H.K. Burnet's arrival at Northbrook saw the installation of a Delplace chamber, the first in this country. This thirty-foot-high, horse-shoe-shaped chamber made use of the sulphur gases given off by the burnt pyrites. Here, Nelson and his brother Fred Sutcliffe stand inside the huge chamber in 1902.

Air Raid, 1940. Leathers Chemical Co. was one of the few Bradford firms to suffer from enemy action during the Second World War, there being only one minor raid on the city on 30 August 1940. Fortunately, only the packing department (seen here) was destroyed; the rest of the plant went unscathed. The release of several hundred tons of sulphuric acid into the environment would not have been pleasant. Here, John Cornwell assesses the damage the following day.

Not everybody worked in the major Bradford industries of wool, coal, stone, and chemicals. On these two pages is a selection of people at work in the city. Above: the 'daily drop'. Draymen deliver beer to the vaults of a corner pub in Leeds Road in 1911. Below: butchers at work in the 74 open stalls of the Rawson Place Market in 1920.

A Bradford chimney sweep, *c.* 1890.

A newspaper vendor sells his wares in George Street as a tram passes down Leeds Road into the city centre.

Farm labourers at rest. In spite of Bradford's status as a large industrial city, in 1900 there were still many people who made their living off the land, particularly in dairy farming. Here, a group of farm workers at Tong have 'drinkings'.

Bridge Street Horse Fair, 1860. Traditionally, Bradford's ancient horse fair was held on the day of St Andrew the Apostle. This was one of the last horse fairs because when in 1866 they purchased the manorial rights, the council prohibited street fairs. Here, local farmers and dealers seem overrun by horses and trading must have been good. Certainly the cobblestones would have been heavily strewn with the best of garden manure. What damage it did to the ladies' ankle-length skirts or the men's shiny boots, only these Victorians could tell us.

Nine
Church and Chapel

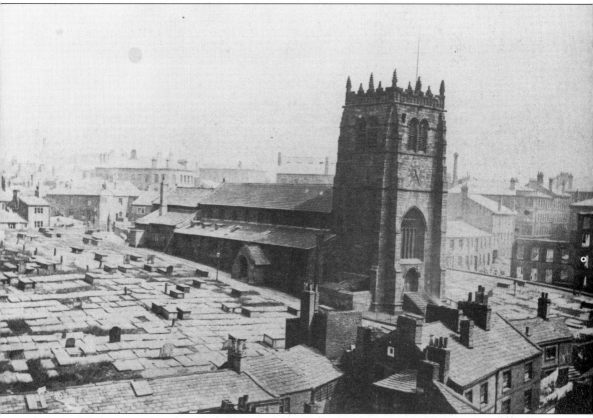

Parish Church, 1900. Despite the popularity of nonconfirmity, the Anglican church continued to play an important part in the spiritual and social welfare of the town. Here, the pinnacles and battlements surmounting the short heavy tower of the church have become blackened by decades of city smoke. During the twentieth century there has been much restoration and extension, particularly to the east end (1958–63). Also, two low western transepts were completed in 1954 to the design of the architect Sir Edward Maufe, who was responsible for Guildford Cathedral. In 1919 the parish church became the cathedral of the Bradford diocese.

Eastbrook Chapel, *c.* 1890. Following John Wesley's first visit to Bradford in 1744 came the foundation of a Methodist Society. The number of Methodist worshippers in Bradford quickly increased, leading to the erection of a chapel in Kirkgate in 1811. However, by 1825 the chapel featured in this photograph had become the main centre of worship for Bradford Methodists. It was located in part of the Peckover estate (in a semi-rural position) at the bottom of Leeds Road. It was designed by Joseph Balham of Sheffield in a plain Gothic style. Here, a meeting of the Methodist Conference takes place in the 1890s and delegates assemble around the graveyard of the chapel.

Eastbrook Hall, 1904. For twenty years the structure of the old chapel was considered unsafe. In the autumn of 1899 it was so dangerous that it was abandoned. It was decided to demolish the old building and move the bodies interred in the chapel burial ground to the West Bowling cemetery. In its place was erected a magnificent New Hall seating 2,000 persons and covering an area of 4,000 square yards. The total cost of the Hall was £21,000. Here, the Hall is opened in March 1904 by Mr and Mrs Oddy (centre) of Birkenshaw.

The move to new premises coincided with the decision at Conference in 1901 to run Eastbrook on Mission lines, separating it from the rest of the circuit. As a result, Revd H.M. Nield succeeded Revd John Wilson as superintendent. Nield introduced a more crusading missionary zeal to get through to the '100,000 people living within 15 minutes walk of the hall'. Nield left Bradford in 1911.

The Wesleyan Chariot, 1905. As part of Eastbrook's new missionary approach, Mr Nield pioneered this portable pulpit for his open-air gospel work. Other successful missionary work was conducted at weekly meetings in Morley Street and in front of the Bradford Wool Exchange.

Apart from the huge auditorium of the new hall, the Eastbrook premises fronting Leeds Road were taken up by shops and offices. At the rear of the hall (with an entrance in Chapel Street) was the Sunday School where thousands of working-class children could find a pleasant, useful and sociable outlet for their free Sunday time. By 1914, Sunday schools had become a key feature of working-class town life with their anniversaries, prize-givings, choral concerts and public parades. The weekly attendance on the Sabbath encouraged children, like these at Eastbrook, into routines of cleanliness, punctuality, good manners, and self-discipline. For harassed working-class parents living in overcrowded houses, they provided a welcome respite from parental responsibilities. Here, young boys and girls from Leeds Road and Vicar Lane are shown a caring attitude in their reading of Bible stories. Below, the privileged children of the area enjoy an anniversary tea while Mr Nield and senior members of the chapel look on.

While Mr Nield's Eastbrook Brotherhood appealed to the artisan and middle-class male, he also tried to reach out to the city's semi-respectable unskilled working-class man. Here, a group of less than enthusiastic Bradford lads appear reluctant to give up their usual pleasures (shove-halfpenny board, to the left) for a proselytizing magic lantern show, while Mr Nield looks on. However, Nield's open-air Temperance Crusade of 1905 was so effective that several Bradford publicans demanded a revision of their poor rates on the grounds that 'the Eastbrook Brotherhood had robbed them of their customers'.

Cottage Services, c. 1914. For working-class women, tied to the hearth and home, Eastbrook's mission was prepared to visit their back street homes and in the top photograph Sister Annie Jackson spreads the gospel in a house in Jermyn Street with hymns from a portable organ.

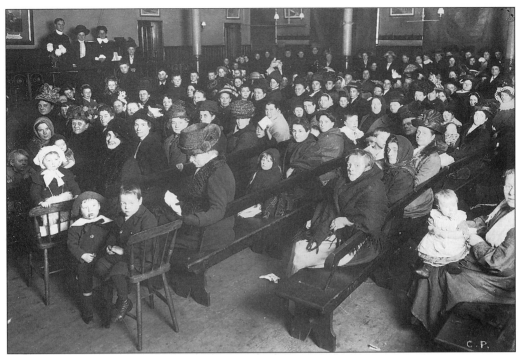

Mothers and toddlers attend the Hall for a weekly service especially for them.

People's entertainment, Southend Hall, 1910. The Methodists in Bradford were quick to spot the persuasive potential of the magic lantern show, and here on the wet cobblestones of Leeds Road in 1910 members of Southend Hall tempt members of the public into Revd Prunell's pictorial address with scenes from the Pilgrim's Progress. The young sinners on the right seem unimpressed.

Ten
Bradford at Play

After 1880, within the church and the chapels (of all denominations), there was as we have seen a systematic effort to cater for all interests and to develop specific religious services to suit specific social groups, for example men only services and sermons for mothers and toddlers. The aim was to transform the church/chapel into a social centre in order to combat the threat from a wave of new mass leisure pursuits, but drink continued to be the old enemy of the church and chapel.

New Inn, Tyrrell Street, 1940. The venue of Bradford's first flower show in 1821, this old pub became a favourite resort of small contractors, waste dealers, and diverse other tradespeople. By the mid-twentieth century when this photograph was taken, the late Peter Holdsworth could describe it as having a 'reputation for naughty lasses but first class ale'. In the background on the far right is the tower of the New Victoria cinema opened in 1930 (now the Odeon).

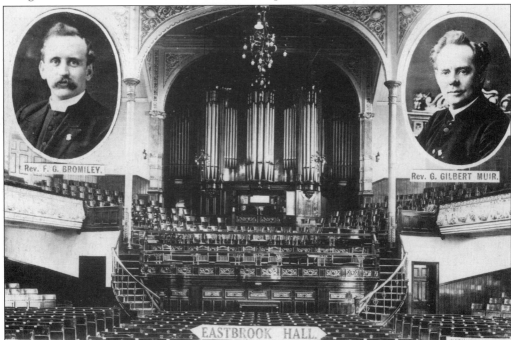

Eastbrook organ. It was during the nineteenth century that West Yorkshire established its reputation as a centre of excellence in choral music with many local chapels competing to produce the best *Messiah* at Christmas time. Here is the organ and auditorium of the Eastbrook Hall, shortly before the First World War.

Street Band. More secular music came initially with the street bands like this one bringing a welcome break to the routine of street life, and though their music lacked instrumental perfection they were big on volume and 'oompah' jollity, often tempting residents into singalongs or impromptu clog dancing. One wonders about the impact of the clarinet played by the youngest member of the band, up against the brass of two cornets, three euphoniums, and a tuba.

Dick Hudson's. Most industrial cities had their escape routes from the long hours at work and the monotony of endless back-to-back terraced houses. Many Bradfordians after 1880 favoured Shipley Glen and Ilkley Moor. By name, this is the Fleece Inn at High Eldwick, but it was better known to most Bradfordians as Dick Hudsons as they poured out of the city like lemmings each Good Friday or Whit Monday. A bank holiday visit to the watering spa of Ilkley via Rombalds Moor was enriched by the gourmet delights of dinner and tea at Dick Hudsons, a half-way house in each direction; best English beef and Yorkshire puddings at lunchtime, and an enormous helping of ''am 'n' eggs' on the return journey. Here a young cyclist is about to resume his journey after his refreshment.

Works trip, 1899. The coming of the railways in the 1840s enabled employees to transport large numbers of people for a day out of the industrial town and cities. In 1849, Titus Salt was one of the first Bradford millowners to reward his employees with a visit to Skipton. Here, Christopher Pratt, furniture makers, treat their staff to a day at Bolton Abbey in 1899 – strictly Sunday best, and not a flat cap in sight!

Charabanc trip, 1924. Motor transport transformed the face of English society after 1918. Like the train excursions of the previous century, the 'chara' trip became a holiday experience in itself, with communal singing, kissing on the back seat, and a 'whip round' for the driver. Here, the employees of G.H. Leather, sulphuric acid manufacturers, take their employees to the British Empire Exhibition at Wembley in 1924.

Bradford Super-Mare, *c.* 1910. This is the promenade at Morecambe before 1914. Morecambe was known as Bradford by the Sea for the number of Bradford folk who holidayed there. Bradford working-class families queued in their thousands at the Midland Station for excursion trains to Morecambe, particularly on the August Saturday of Bowling Tide week.

Bradfordians on the beach. Seaside visits to the east coast at Scarborough were less popular with Bradfordians, but it was a Bradford newsagent and bookseller, William Morgan, who saw the commercial opportunities of a pleasurable visit to the seaside. After building the Winter Gardens at Blackpool and Morecambe he invested £6,000 in building the People's Palace and Aquarium at Scarborough. Here, day trippers to Scarborough enjoy the more traditional Punch and Judy show on the beach and turn their backs on Morgan's fun palace.

Southend Hall Gymnastics Club, 1901. The Methodist boys' gymnastics club of Southend Hall – a good example of the muscular Christianity movement of the late nineteenth century.

Bradford Billiard Hall, 1904. Young men from Laisterdyke in Bradford play a game of billiards at Southend Hall. Traditionally, this had been an upper-class, male pursuit, enjoyed in wealthy houses only.

Bradford Ramblers, 1911. Up to 1930, Whitsuntide marked the beginning of the summer season, with the first visits to the seaside and the traditional Sunday school 'walks' or field days. In the north of England, by 1914, there was an increase in outdoor recreational activity. Enjoying the fresh air of the Yorkshire moors became an obsession with the Bradford rambling fraternity. J.B. Priestley noted of Bradford prior to 1914 that 'Everybody went on enormous walks. I

have known men who thought nothing of tramping between 30 and 40 miles every Sunday'. This Edwardian family takes a breather on the limestone outcrop of a Dales hillside.

Bradford's Whit Walk 1959. More formal, competitive walking or pedestrianism was taken up by amateur athletic clubs in the last quarter of the nineteenth century. The Yorkshire Walking Club was formed in June 1912 under the presidency of J. Russel Rose of Bradford. Prior to that, several towns including Bradford had formed associations providing races for club members. The Bradford Whit Walk was first held in 1903 over a 40-mile course, taking in Tadcaster and York. Since 1945, the course has been a circular one of 31 miles taking in Mid-Airdale and Wharfedale. In those post-war days the event aroused great interest among Bradford's Whit Monday holidaymakers. Here the race starts in Bank Street in 1959. On the extreme left (no. 6) is Albert Johnson (Sheffield United), who dominated the event throughout the 1950s, winning every year but one from 1954 to 1963.

Horton Park, *c.* 1900. A major feature of the new industrial towns like Bradford was the lack of open space. During the 1860s, due to growing civic pride and private philanthropy, Bradford did much to remedy this situation by providing public open spaces in the shape of municipal parks. The first of these was at Peel Park in 1863 and fifteen years later the park here at Horton was opened by Major Briggs Priestley. Within its 39 acres were two ornamental lakes, three bowling greens, one putting green, eight tennis courts, and a children's corner.

BAND STAND, LISTER PARK, BRADFORD.   P. 154.

Brass Band, Lister Park, *c.* 1914. Yorkshire's numerous brass bands became a feature of religious parades, political meetings, and sporting occasions but they are perhaps best remembered for their playing in the public parks on a Sunday afternoon in summer. Here, Sunday strollers in Lister Park in 1914 are serenaded by the strains of a slow melody played by any one of dozens of local brass bands.

Princes Theatre, Little Horton Lane. Until its closure in 1961 this was a favourite with Bradford's theatre-going public. It had been launched in 1876 by William Morgan, an early Bradford impresario. In 1878 it was devastated by fire but restored by Henry Pullan and, later, Francis Laidler, Bradford's 'King of Pantomime'. For most of this century it provided a home for good repertory theatre and premiered several of Priestley's early plays. Until 1938 it shared the site with the People's Palace, formerly the Star Music Hall. The entrance to the music hall was down the side street on the right.

Empire Theatre, Great Horton Road, c. 1914. This was one of a chain of successful variety theatres opened by Sir Edward Moss. This one opened in January 1899 and was built onto the back of licensed premises, the Alexandra Hotel. Here, knockabout comedians, female impersonators and pretty female ballad singers entertained the rough and respectable of Bradford's theatre-going public. J.B. Priestley was particularly fond of the 'fourpenny balcony at the Empire'. Following a fire in 1917 the theatre was converted to a cinema.

Alhambra Theatre. In 1914 John Rand's mill was demolished to make way for Francis Laidler's new variety theatre in direct competition with the Moss Empire theatre at the back of the Alexandra Hotel (seen to the right of this picture). It was from the Alhambra that the British National Opera Company was launched in 1922. For the greater part of this century the theatre was best known for its pantomimes.

Theatre Royal. This theatre opened on Boxing Day 1864 as the Royal Alexandra, as there was already a Theatre Royal in Duke Street. It finally took that name in 1868 when its reputation soared under the management of Charles Rice. Most of the principal Victorian stage names appeared here. Lily Langtry performed for just one week in 1882, the very week that the Prince of Wales came to Bradford to open the new Technical College. By 1921 it had been fully converted to a cinema and remained so until the end of its days in 1974, with a showing of *The Graduate*. Next door is the Royal Standard public house and furthest left are the Connaught Rooms.

Theatre Royal, 1905. A view of the same building thirty years earlier in its heyday as a repertory theatre. In fact this photograph was taken by a local theatre manager the day after Henry Irving's death here on Friday 13 October 1905. Irving had been in Bradford all week with a tour of three plays. That night he had managed to complete his performance of *Becket* with the final line of the play – 'Into thy hands, O Lord. Into thy hands … '. The Victorian stage superstar staggered off the stage and was taken by cab a few hundred yards to his suite at the Midland Hotel where he collapsed and died in the foyer. Here, the flag is at half mast; the billboards have been blanked out and his business manager Bram Stoker (of *Dracula* fame) is about to cross the road (with umbrella) having announced the sad news to the rest of the company.

Henry Irving and the Theatre Royal. Within hours the entire nation was in mourning for the 67-year-old actor. An omen of the tragedy was in the posters all around the town that week, which read 'Farewell of Henry Irving' and should have read 'Farewell Tour of Henry Irving'. The printers realised their mistake but went ahead with the publication. The following night the body was supposed to leave Bradford's Exchange Station in secret but thousands of mourners lined the route from the hotel in absolute silence.

New Victoria Cinema, *c.* 1935. Bradford men had done much to pioneer the creation of the moving film during the 1890s but the real cinema boom came from across the Atlantic in the 1920s and 1930s. This splendid new cinema was built (with two million bricks) in 1930 on the site of an old brewery. It contained a cafe and ballroom and its huge auditorium could house 3,318 people. The cinema had a 'Mighty Wurlitzer' organ.

Odeon Cinema, Manchester Road, *c.* 1960. This cinema opened in 1939, shortly before the Second World War, with a world premiere of *The Ware Case*. By that time there were 42 cinemas open in the Bradford area. Despite some war damage the cinema served Bradford well until its closure in 1969. Next door is the Oddfellows Arms.

The Ritz, Broadway, 1947. This innovative cinema design of W.R. Glen never did fit comfortably with the smoke-blackened warehouses and arcades of the city centre. it was opened in May 1939 by Major T. Robinson and housed a cinema organ until damaged by flooding in the 1950s. Admittance was originally by both Leeds Road and Broadway, but the former entrance gave way to a row of shops and restaurants. Opening on the very eve of the Second World War, the Ritz became an escapists' delight as Errol Flynn, Veronica Lake, Victor Mature, and Hedy Lamarr lightened the dark days for a few hours each evening. In the centre of the photograph at the large street junction beyond the cinema is Monkman's corner, where young teenagers arranged to rendezvous with their cinema 'date'. This was the site not only for sweethearts to meet but was probably the favourite meeting place in the whole city for families, friends, hikers, theatregoers, etc., to meet up together.

Bradford City, F.A. Cup winners, 1911. This success came only eight seasons after their formation and following promotion from Division Two in 1908. Forty thousand Bradfordians had watched City beat Burnley in the quarter-final at Valley Parade. A surprise 3–0 victory over Blackburn Rovers gave them a place in the final against Cup favourites Newcastle United. Supporters from eleven excursion trains were disappointed by a goalless draw at Crystal Palace. The replay at Old Trafford the following Wednesday saw City captain Jimmy Spiers head in the game's only goal. Over the two games, 137,000 spectators had attended. Here, the victorious City team with their giant goalkeeper, Mark Mellors, and player/manager, Peter O'Rourke, pose before the Valley Parade grandstand which burnt down so tragically in 1985. Spiers, the goalscorer, is seated immediately left of the F.A. Cup. The team are sporting the famous claret jerseys with amber yoke.

Crag Road United, 1926–7. At the amateur level, thousands of young Bradford men played soccer in the inter-war years. Here is the very successful Crag Road team of 1926/7, which played in the Bradford Amateur League and in the 1920s won the Bradford Hospital Cup, Amateur Cup, and Bradford and District Cup. Founded in 1921 by a bunch of lads 'wi' nowt to do' they obtained the support and sponsorship of George Ricks, a Bradford publican.

Bradford Northern R.F.C. with the Rugby League Cup, 1947.

Bradford Northern's Cup Triumph at Wembley in 1947. Northern made three consecutive appearances in the Wembley Final between 1947–49. Here, we see them victorious in the first of those games. Skipper Ernest Ward holds the trophy aloft after an 8–4 win over neighbours Leeds. Willie Davies (second from right), Northern's Welsh international stand-off, won the Lance Todd trophy for man of the match. The takings were £17,483 from the crowd of 78,000 who paid to watch the game. In the following year Northern lost the final to Wigan but returned to defeat Halifax 12–0 in 1949.

Eleven

Watch the Birdie

'Watch the birdie', c. 1865. The invention of photography in the mid-nineteenth century and the emergence of the professional photographer and his studio had far-reaching consequences for our Victorian and Edwardian forebears. More so for us today, who are able to see them as they were, at work and play, on wedding days and special occasions. Here, at Horse Close Bridge in Norwood Green John o'Judy examines a very early camera.

Plate Camera of Christopher Pratt, Bradford, 1904. By 1900 the plate camera and its accessories had become much more sophisticated. Here is the quarter plate camera and tripod with bellows belonging to young Christopher Pratt, a member of the successful furniture manufacturing business in North Parade, Bradford. With this camera he captured several of the images in this book, particularly those relating to the work of the Methodists of Eastbrook Hall, where his parents and grandparents were lifelong worshippers.

Photographic Studio, Barkerend Road, c. 1895. In 1885, Alfred Coe, a gifted painter of portraits, had started in business in these premises in Barkerend Road. During the 1890s this talented photographer took out patents on collotype printing machinery, employing over forty people in his large workshop in Vicar Lane. His three daughters and a son all appear to have taken an active part in the business.

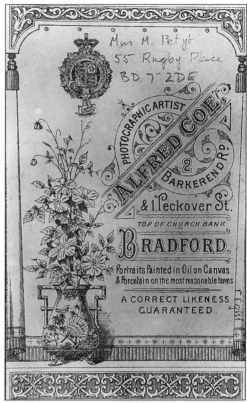

This is the reverse of a carte-de-visite by Coe and is typical of many photographers' trade cards of the period. By 1898 Coe had spotted the commercial potential in the correspondence card, better known as the picture poscard, which became increasingly popular in the Edwardian era. A wide variety of themes and items were used to illustrate the cards – sporting and political events, local views and personalities.

Photographic Society outing, 1916. By 1910, photography had become a popular pastime with enthusiastic amateurs, and here the Bradford Photographic Society pose on the annual excursion to Hawksworth in 1916. By this time Alfred Coe had sold his very successful business and had emigrated to America, where he died in 1917.

Coe's Postcards, *c.* 1902. Here are two examples of Coe's prolific output of postcards and comic cards between 1895 and 1905. In 1903 he had produced a successful series of reproductions of water-colour paintings of old Bradford and a year later his company exploited the Bradford Exhibition to the full. In the top photograph, Coe has captured a 'tingleary' man in Peckover Street, and below, a view up Barkerend Road from outside Coe's photographic studio on the right.

Twelve
The Daily Round

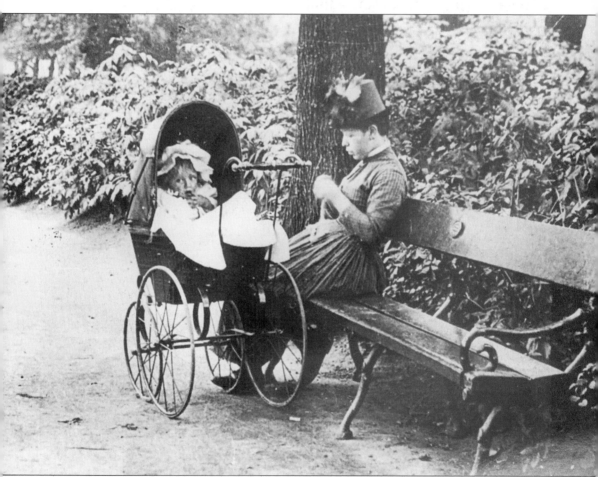

A Bradford Nanny, 1901. This final section of the book is devoted to those day-in-day-out routines of the people of Bradford over the past one hundred years. We begin with a young nanny and her charge in Lister Park in 1901. This was a favourite haunt of nursemaids and nannies from the well-to-do homes in the Hallfield and Thorncliffe estates as well as from the magnificent residences in and around Manningham Lane and St Paul's Road.

A Bradford Yard, 1910. Bradford's Edwardian working class helped each other to get through the daily round. Families little better off than each other came to the help of neighbours when times were hard, although living 'on top of each other' did not always lead to friendship and a cosy community spirit, as some writers would have us believe. Here, the snow has been cleared in the communal alley and the frying pan is poised. Perhaps it is Pancake Day?!

Family Life, c. 1900. Outside the city streets, life could be just as grim for those in the suburbs and the countryside. This scene of domestic bliss may have been the exception. They are all well-clothed and their feet well shod. The window panes positively gleam and the kitchen garden has been well tended. The exact location of this Bradford scene is not known.

Bradford Garden Party, 1906. For the middle and artisan classes Bradford's process of industrialisation had brought only benefits. On a sunny day in 1906, these better-off folk of the city take afternoon tea.

Spice Market, *c.* 1950. To the right is the flower stall of Messrs Badlands which faced the market shoppers once he had climbed the wide stone stairs of the Kirkgate entrance to Kirkgate Market. In the corner is a favourite toy shop of the author's, where grandma often spoiled me with a lead soldier or a Dinky car. In later life, the second-hand bookshop of Fred Power was always a magnet, the sheet music stall not far away and numerous cosy cafés selling pie and peas, tripe and onions, cornish pasty and chips, and other northern delicacies for a cold winter's Saturday.

St James' Markets, 1920. A completely different kind of market, St James' wholesale markets for fruit and vegetables, and the meat market, both of which played a crucial part in the distribution of the city's food. The fruit market and abattoirs had opened in 1871 and three years later the fruit market was opened for market garden produce brought directly into the market via an adjoining railway siding of the Great Northern line.

Wool sorting, c. 1935. The wool textile industry shared in the depression of the inter-war years. The local rate of unemployment reached a peak of 20 per cent in 1936. Even for the skilled woolsorter there was short time and piece work.

A mashin' of tea. Bradford's Edwardian poor certainly helped each other. Families came to the aid of neighbours in need without a thought of reward. Here, a cup of sugar or a mashing of tea has been borrowed from some kindly neighbour.

Eviction! *c.* 1900. A familiar scene in Bradford streets before the First World War. Deserted by the father, a family like this was not many weeks away from total destitution and the workhouse. In most cases, mothers, aged before their time with continuous child-bearing, were too dependent to become the bread-winner overnight. Many were ignorant, not only of worldly matters but of personal hygiene and even the rudiments of babycare.

Mill Girls, 1908. Two mill girls from Mount Street mill, Leeds Road, pose for amateur photographer Christopher Pratt in 1908. Their brief childhood is almost at an end as they hover on the threshold of womanhood, innocently unshawled; a working-class woman, even if she slipped next door, would not do so without her shawl. To be seen in public uncovered provoked street gossip and a reputation for indecency.

Begging in the streets *c*. 1905. According to government statistics, only 90 people died of 'starvation or privation due to destitution' in the England of 1912! This misleading and conservative figure does not reflect the large numbers who were forced to beg on the streets for survival. Here, some youngsters pester a well-to-do gentleman in George Street – or is it something more sinister? By 1917, the numbers of those under 21 committed for prostitution had risen by 54 per cent. The governor at Liverpool prison reported that a large proportion of convicted prostitutes in the port were 'mere children'. No doubt Bradford had its similar problems.

Dancing bear, 1908. The Bradford street in Edwardian times offered a variety of entertainments apart from music. Here, a dancing bear entertains a small crowd in Peckover Street in 1908.

Washday! Despite the smoke and grime of the city, most Bradfordians tried to keep themselves and their possessions clean. Some housewives gave up their lives to domesticity, polishing furniture, black leading fire irons, and, on Mondays – washing. Here, all the technology of a working-class washday: mangle, peggy tub, posser and, out of sight, a large bar of carbolic soap.

Chimney Sweep, c. 1930. Wet clothes were usually dried on 'clothes horses' around the fire, most of which were coal fired. The chimneys required the periodical sweep, and here a Bradford sweep is distracted by an interested onlooker.

Advertising. Before the age of television's commercial break, stores advertised themselves and their goods in a variety of ways. John S. Driver, general grocer and greengrocer, certainly goes to great lengths in this pre-1914 sales campaign in Forster Square. From their headquarters in Ingleby Road and numerous branches throughout Bradford, Driver's supplied cheap but quality foodstuffs. During the hard times of the 1930s, thousands of Bradforians were thankful for the 'Driver Parcel' of a rabbit, one onion, a carrot, a small turnip, and a few potatoes – all for a shilling!

Outdoor department, Seymour Street, 1904. In Victorian families where a wife had put her foot down and demanded a share in the 'good life', husband or wife might obtain a jug of beer from the 'outdoor department' of the local pub, or from the local off licence. Here, in Seymour Street, Leeds Road, a father is about to leave the premises of George Popplewell with a jug of ale to be drunk at home. Men who did not visit pubs or drank at home were sneered at by their peers as 'hen-pecked', or 'miseries'.

Street corner, 1904. Older boys and young men gather at a Bradford street corner in 1904 to insult the girls and scorn the respectful. The members of such a gang as this had usually left school and worked part-time by running errands for building labourers, millworkers, or foundrymen.

A Bradford square, c. 1911. Bradford's Edwardian working-class parents regarded it as a natural right that children should go out to work as early as possible to compensate them for the kept years of childhood. But it was good while it lasted, and most people look back with fondness upon the street games and songs they enjoyed as children. Here, the towering backcloth of the mill and its chimney and the proximity of the terraced houses creates a natural and safe playground for this gang of Bradford youngsters. The gang had its own unwritten constitution and membership rules with a clearly marked territory, trespass upon which provoked gang wars.

Bill poster, 1895. Hoardings like this one in Buttershaw and numerous others seen in this selection of Bradford photographs were a common feature of the Edwardian street, where gable ends were smothered by numerous advertisements for boot polish, liver pills, and theatre shows. In fact, such hoardings were a great help to many children of the lower classes in shaking off their illiteracy. They often brought a touch of humour and vitality to the dark, grimy bulks of Victorian architecture and to the monotony of the urban streets.

Street Cutler, *c.* 1890. A familiar sight in Bradford streets before the First World War was the knife and scissors grinder, Tommy Masterson, here watched by a smart young lad who perhaps awaits his mother's best carving knife.

Forster Square, *c.* 1914. A favourite photograph of the author's which seems to epitomize that prosperous, busy, and industrious city of the Edwardian era. The Saltaire tram is about to depart Forster Square at a busy 'home time'. I would be a rich man indeed had I a pound for every flat cap in view. As the public buildings of a modern industrial Bradford surround its citizens, the solid grandeur of its ancient church tower looms over all, to remind us of the town's long history and deep traditions.

Acknowledgements

The greater part of this collection of pictures has come to the author through the generosity of friends and students who have given, or loaned for copying, treasured family photographs. In particular, I should like to record my gratitude to: Christopher and David Pratt, Keith Davies, David Burnet, Dorothy Burrows, Mabel Bruce, Kenneth Firth, Gordon Hodgson, Graham Hall, Frank Woodall, and Malcolm Hitt.

My thanks are also due to Bradford Libraries and Museums Service and Bradford *Telegraph & Argus* for their permission to reproduce several images from their respective collections. A special thank-you to Ian Ward, for photographic expertise, and to Wendy Tapsell for secretarial assistance.